SYNCOPATION #2
IN THE JAZZ IDIOM FOR THE DRUMSET

Ted Reed

Alfred Music
P.O. Box 10003
Van Nuys, CA 91410-0003
alfred.com

ISBN-10: 0-7390-3455-3
ISBN-13: 978-0-7390-3455-2

Introduction

Many teachers and professional drummers have discovered that, the ways to play PROGRESSIVE STEPS TO SYNCOPATION FOR THE MODERN DRUMMER are endless. However, there are also many that have not made this discovery. With this in mind, the following pages will show five different ways to play just eight pages of this book — pages 37 through 44. There are five sections — each consisting of the solo exercises in these pages.

SECTION I. (pages 5 through 12)
The accented notes for the large and small tom-toms spell out the syncopated rythms in these eight pages. All unaccented notes are played on the snare drum. Bass drum four in each bar. Hi Hat on two and four — not written.

SECTION II. (pages 13 through 20)
The accented notes for the bass drum spell out the syncopated rhythms in these eight pages. The unaccented notes are played on the snare drum — left hand. Top line ride cymbal — right hand. Hi Hat on two and four — not written.

SECTION III. (pages 21 through 28)
The solo line will be played on the snare drum — left hand. Bass drum four in each bar. Top line ride cymbal — right hand. Hi Hat on two and four — not written.

SECTION IV. (pages 29 through 36)
The solo line will be played on the bass drum. Snare drum — left hand — click sound on two and four. Top line ride cymbal — right hand. Hi Hat on two and four — not written.

SECTION V. (pages 37 through 44)
The solo line will be played between the snare drum — left hand — and the bass drum. Top line ride cymbal — right hand. Hi Hat on two and four — not written.

SOLO EXERCISE 1   SECTION I

SECTION I. (pages 5 through 12)
All accented notes are played on the large and small tom-toms.
All unaccented notes are played on the snare drum.
Bass drum four in each bar.
Hi Hat on two and four — not written.

SOLO EXERCISE 2

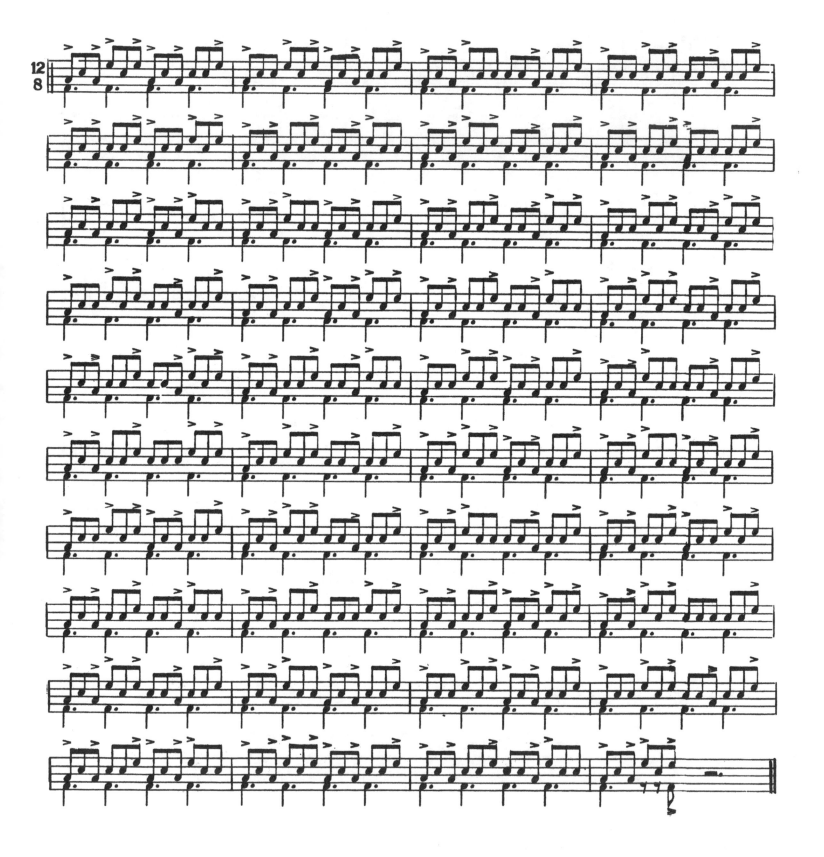

SOLO EXERCISE 3

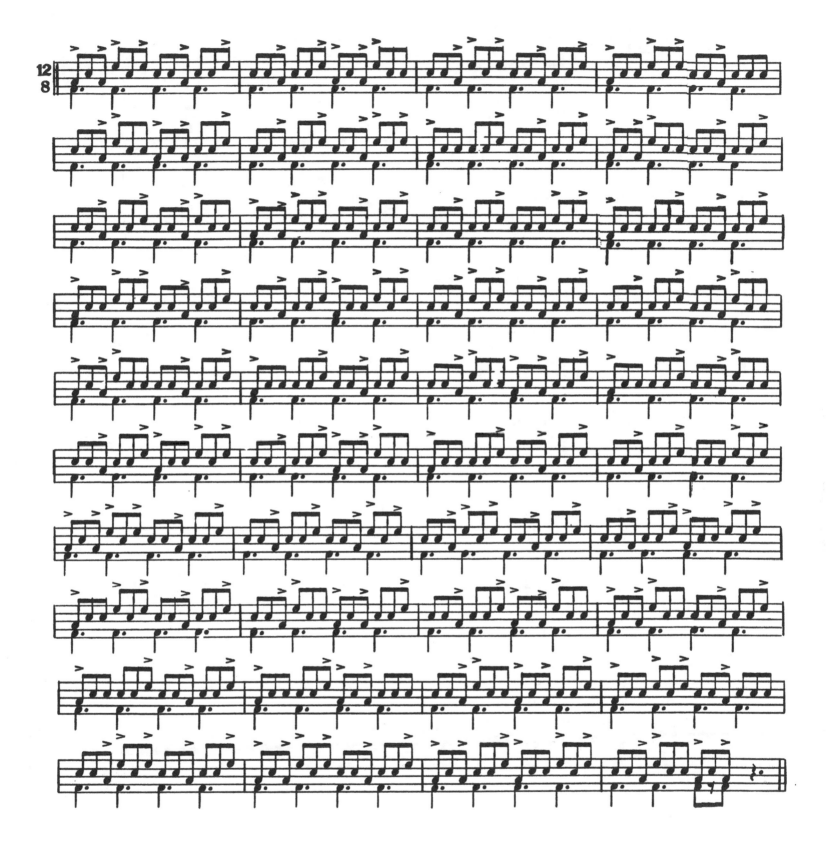

SOLO EXERCISE 4

SOLO EXERCISE 5

SOLO EXERCISE 6

SOLO EXERCISE 7

SOLO EXERCISE 8

SOLO EXERCISE 1   SECTION II

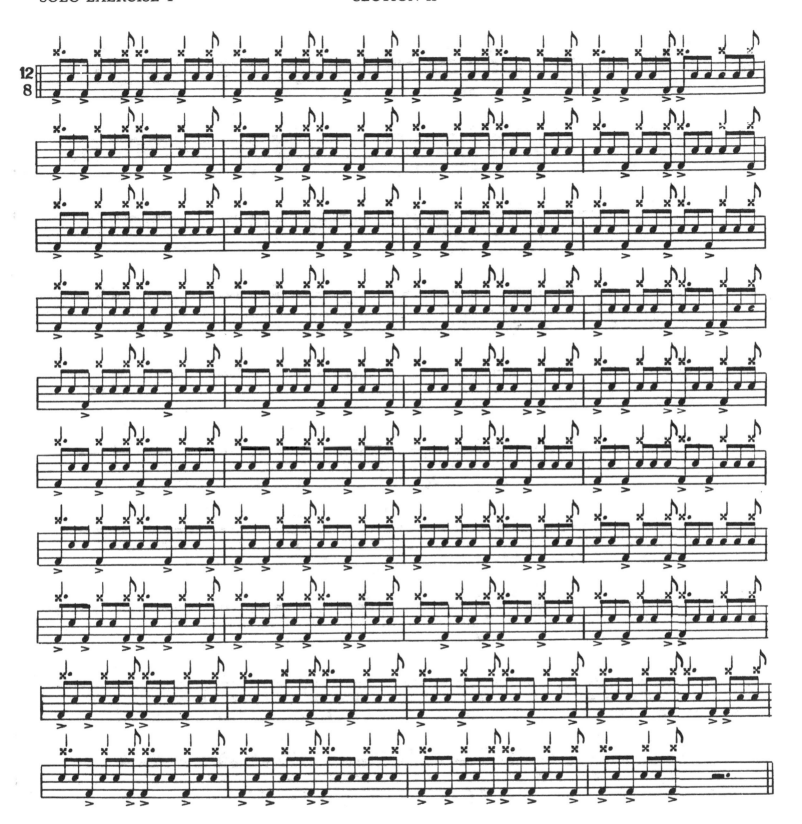

SECTION II. (pages 13 through 20)
All accented notes are played on the bass drum.
All unaccented notes are played on the snare drum — left hand.
Top line ride cymbal — right hand.
Hi Hat on two and four — not written.

SOLO EXERCISE 2

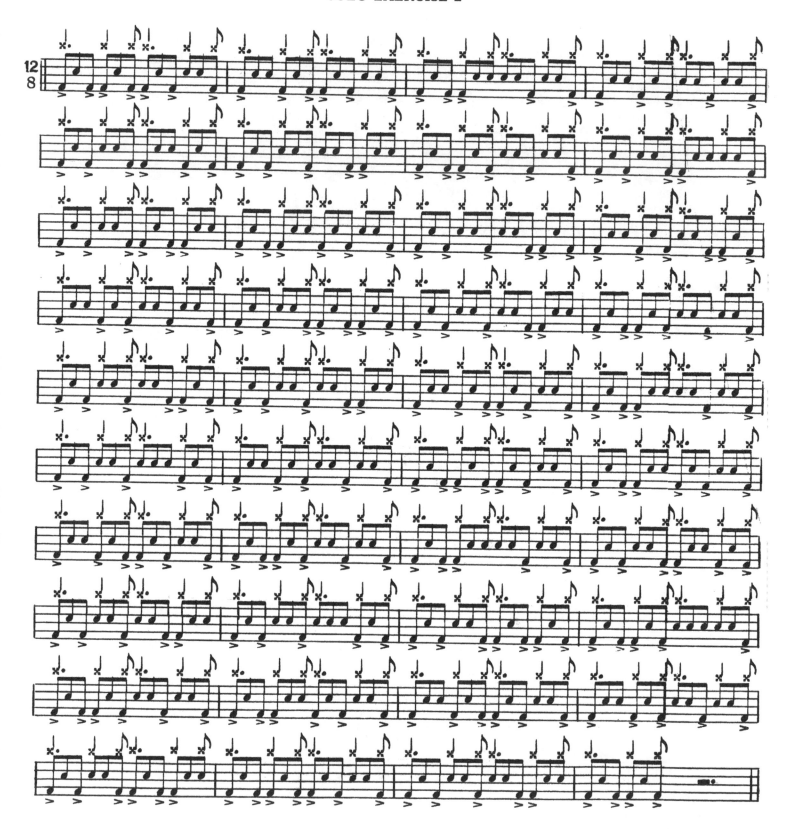

SOLO EXERCISE 3

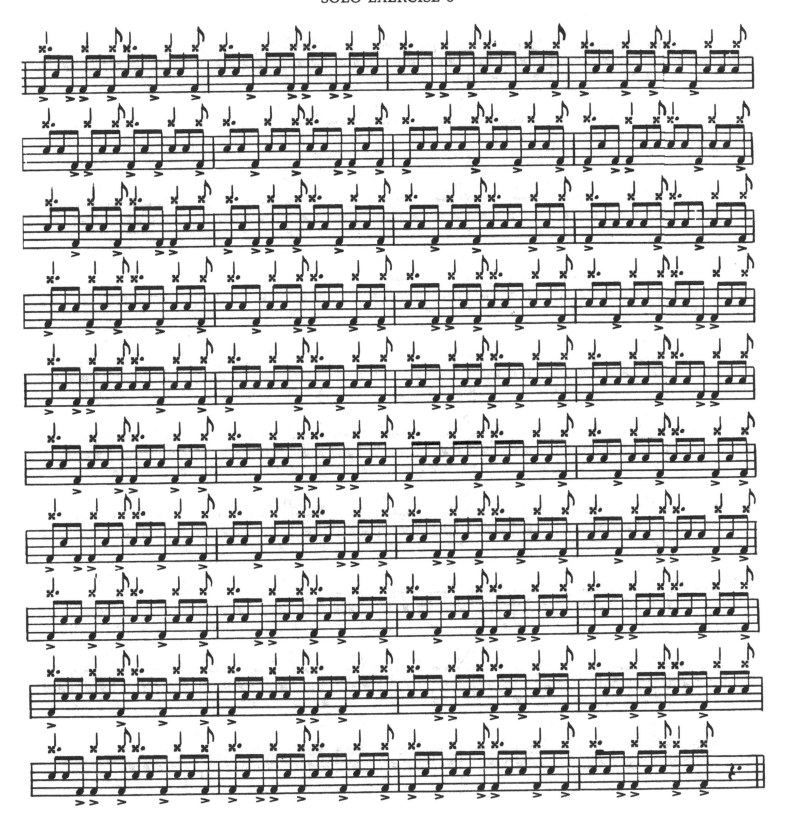

SOLO EXERCISE 4

SOLO EXERCISE 5

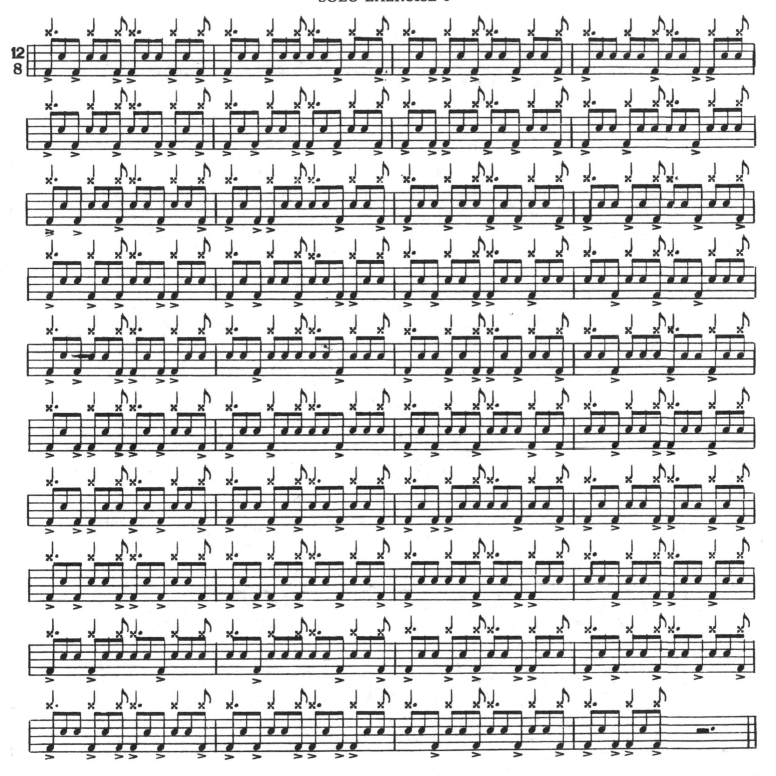

SOLO EXERCISE 6

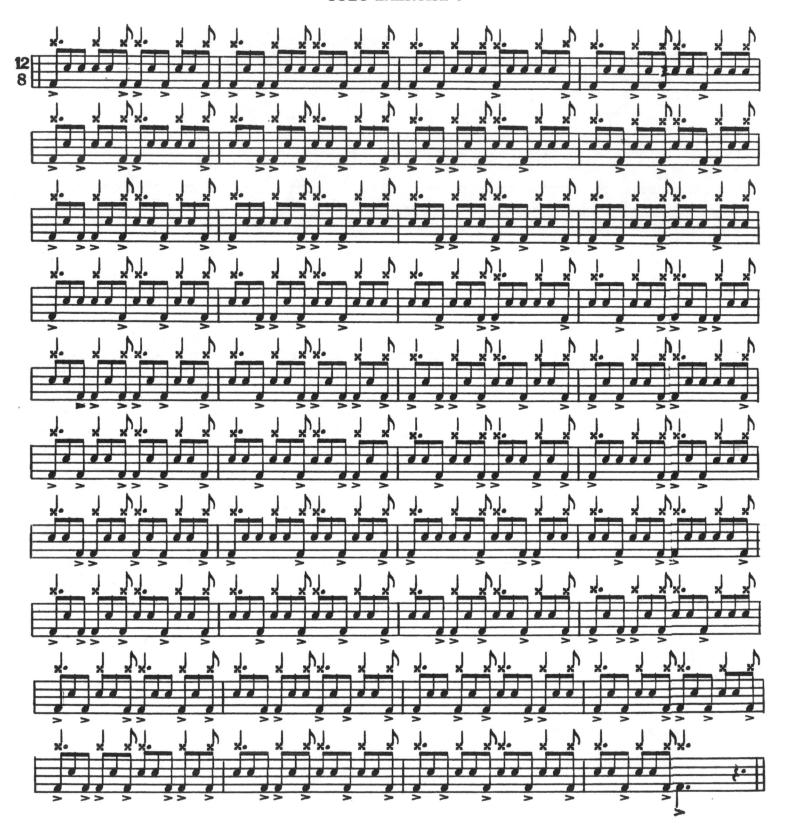

SOLO EXERCISE 7

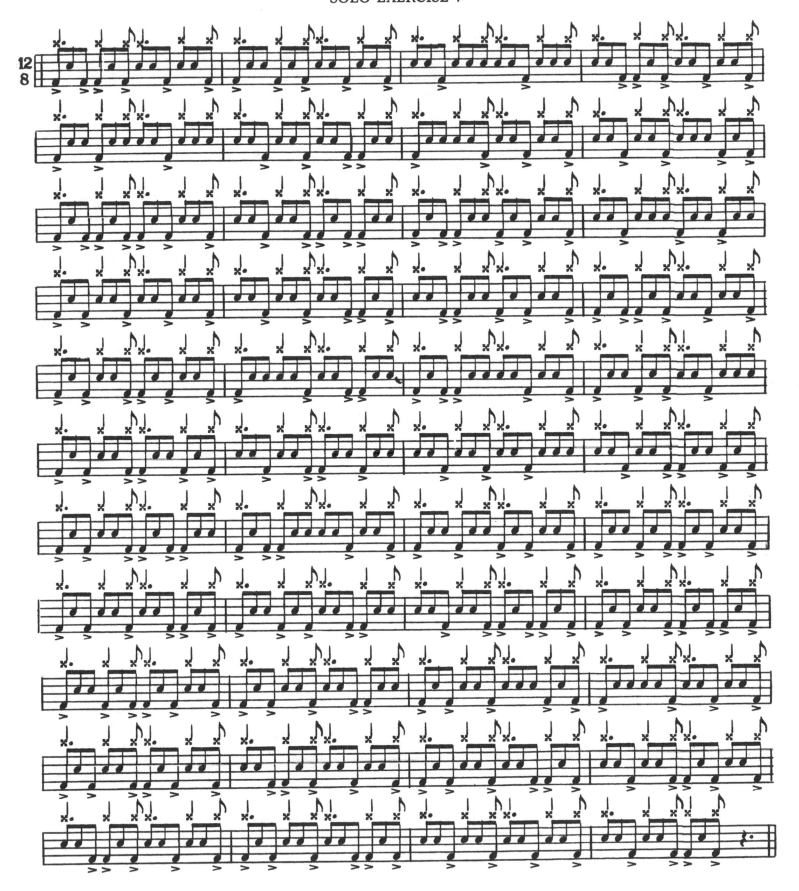

SOLO EXERCISE 8

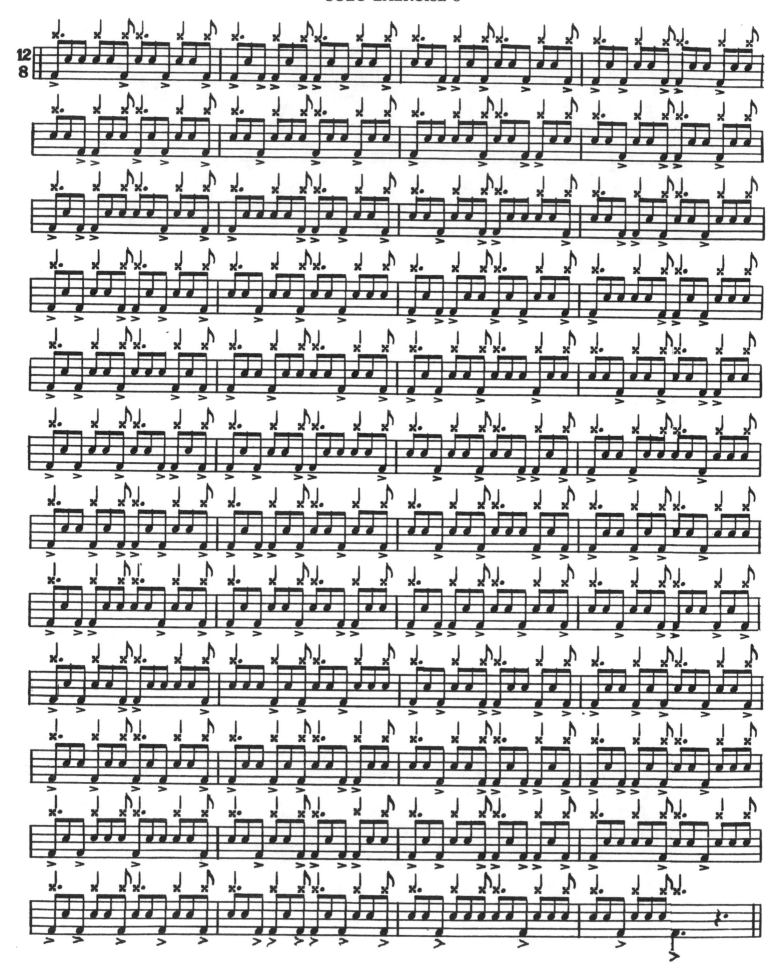

SOLO EXERCISE 1   SECTION III

SECTION III. (pages 21 through 28)
Solo line — snare drum — left hand.
Bass drum four in each bar.
Top line ride cymbal — right hand.
Hi Hat on two and four — not written.

SOLO EXERCISE 2

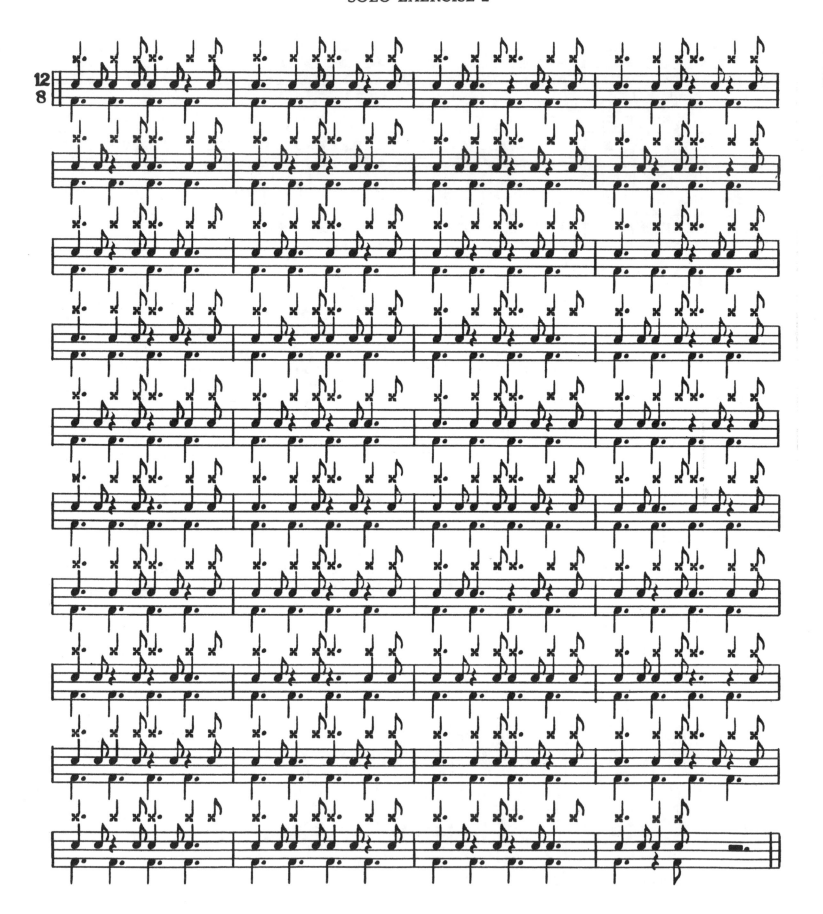

SOLO EXERCISE 3

SOLO EXERCISE 4

SOLO EXERCISE 5

SOLO EXERCISE 6

SOLO EXERCISE 7

SOLO EXERCISE 8

SOLO EXERCISE 1   SECTION IV

SECTION IV. (pages 29 through 36)
Solo line — bass drum.
Snare drum — left hand — click sound on two and four.
Top line ride cymbal — right hand.
Hi Hat on two and four — not written.

SOLO EXERCISE 2

SOLO EXERCISE 3

SOLO EXERCISE 4

SOLO EXERCISE 5

SOLO EXERCISE 6

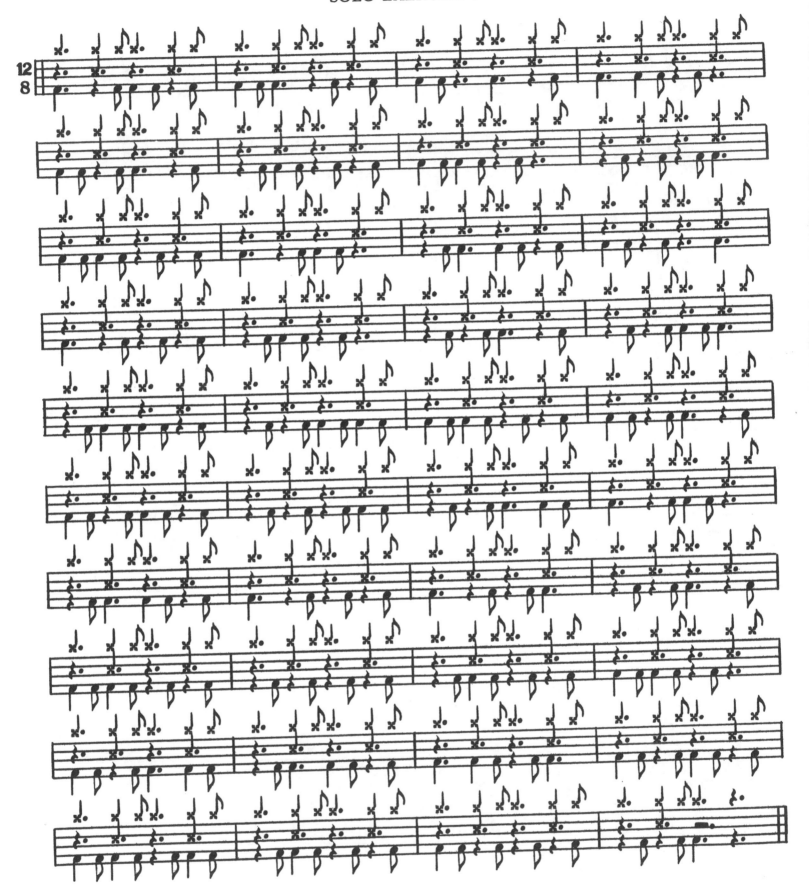

SOLO EXERCISE 7

SOLO EXERCISE 8

SOLO EXERCISE 1 SECTION V

SECTION V. (pages 37 through 44)
The solo line is played between the snare drum —
left hand — and the bass drum.
Top line ride cymbal — right hand.
Hi Hat on two and four — not written.

SOLO EXERCISE 2

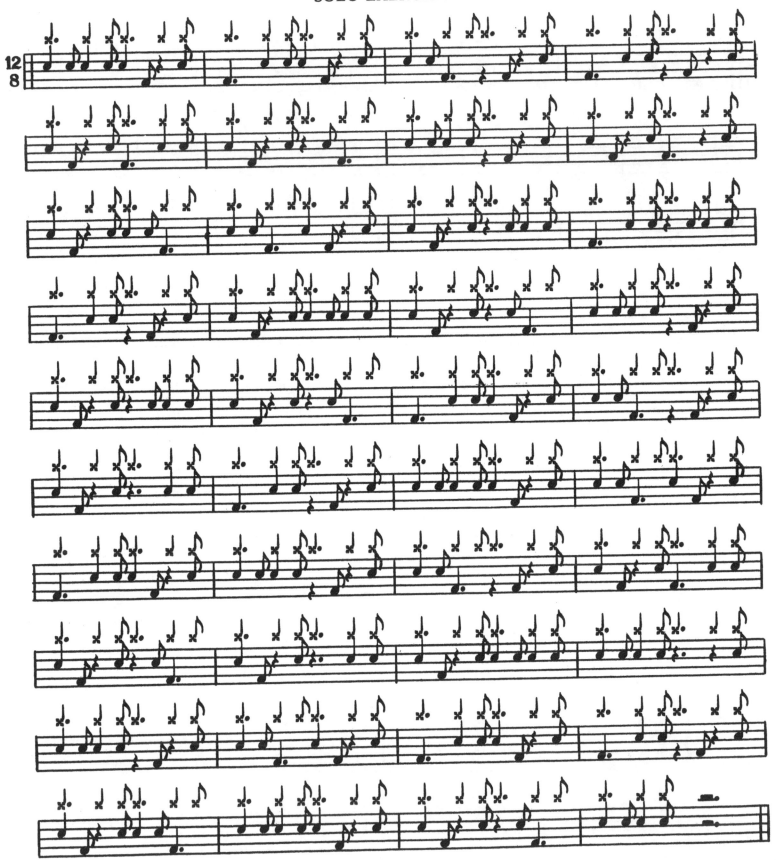

SOLO EXERCISE 3

SOLO EXERCISE 4

SOLO EXERCISE 5

SOLO EXERCISE 6

SOLO EXERCISE 7

SOLO EXERCISE 8